I've Accepted
THE MANTLE,
NOW WHAT?

I've Accepted the Mantle, Now What?

Dr. Leslie Gordon

Copyright © 2024 by Dr. Leslie Gordon
All rights reserved.

No part of this publication may be reproduced, distributed, or transmitted in any form or by any means, including photocopying, recording, or other electronic or mechanical methods, without the prior written permission of the author, except in the case of brief quotations embodied in critical reviews and certain other noncommercial uses permitted by copyright law.

For permission requests, write to the author at:
justlesministries@gmail.com

This book is a work of inspiration and teaching. Any resemblance to actual persons, living or dead, or actual events is purely coincidental.

ISBN: 978-1-960316-40-0

TABLE OF CONTENTS

Copyright

Table of Content

Introduction

Chapter 1:	Examples of Accepted Mantles in the Bible	1
Chapter 2:	Types of Mantles	8
Chapter 3:	The Process Begins-The Downloading Has Begun	17
Chapter 4:	Hearing God's Voice	24
Chapter 5:	When People Don't Understand	32
Chapter 6:	Aligning Yourself with God and His People	39
Chapter 7:	The Importance of a Church Covering	46
Chapter 8:	Obedience Over Trends	54
Chapter 9:	The Attacks of the Enemy	68
Chapter 10:	Fully Accepting the Mantle God Has Placed on You	75

Introduction: Understanding the Mantle

In biblical terms, a "mantle" represents more than a physical garment; it is a profound symbol of the calling, anointing, and responsibility bestowed by God upon an individual to fulfill a specific purpose. Throughout Scripture, the mantle represents God's divine appointment, authority, and empowerment.

The prophet Elijah passed his mantle to Elisha in 2 Kings 2:13-15, signifying the transfer of prophetic authority and responsibility. When Elisha took up Elijah's mantle, it was not just a gesture but a declaration of readiness to walk in a calling that required unwavering faith and commitment. Likewise, Jesus "mantled" His disciples with the Great Commission in Matthew 28:18-20, charging them to spread the Gospel and make disciples of all nations. These examples illustrate that accepting a mantle is not merely about taking on a task but embracing a divine mission with eternal significance.

The Weight and Honor of the Mantle

Accepting a mantle is both a privilege and a responsibility. It means stepping into God's divine plan, carrying the weight of His purpose, and trusting in His provision to fulfill the calling. A mantle is not about personal ambition but about aligning ourselves with God's will and advancing His kingdom.

While the mantle symbolizes God's trust and empowerment, it also comes with challenges. Saying "yes" to God often means walking a path that requires faith, sacrifice, and obedience. The mantle may bring blessings and breakthroughs but will also demand perseverance through trials, resistance, and spiritual warfare. Carrying a mantle acknowledges that you are set apart for a unique purpose that may stretch you beyond your comfort zone but will ultimately glorify God.

Why This Book?

This book is for those who have said "yes" to their mantle and are navigating the complexities of walking in their calling. It is for those who feel the weight of their divine assignment but are unsure what comes next. Perhaps you have experienced doubt, wondering if you aregenuinely equipped for the task. Maybe you have faced opposition, loneliness, or a season of waiting and preparation that feels endless. You are not alone.

Each chapter is designed to guide you through accepting and carrying your mantle. You will learn from biblical examples of individuals who embraced their callings, sometimes reluctantly, but ultimately fulfilled God's purpose for their lives. You will discover the importance of hearing God's voice, aligning yourself with His will, and persevering through challenges. You will be encouraged to trust in God's timing and to understand that the journey is as much about refining your character as it is about fulfilling your calling.

A Personal Invitation

I know the reality of this journey because I have walked it myself. Saying "yes" to God is transformative, but it is not without its trials. My acceptance of the mantle has included moments of spiritual attacks and unexpected challenges, including a hospital stay that resulted in two surgeries in less than two weeks. However, through every challenge, I have witnessed God's faithfulness. The enemy may try to derail God's plans, but he cannot stop them.

I have learned that accepting your mantle means committing to being a willing vessel for God, no matter what. It means being available, obedient, and ready to be used by Him, even when the path is unclear. This book invites you to join me on this journey, to embrace the mantle God has placed on your life, and to trust Him through every season.

Stepping Into the Journey

The journey of carrying a mantle is one of transformation. It will challenge you, refine you, and strengthen your relationship with God. You may face moments of loneliness, quiet times, fasting, and prayer as God prepares you for what lies ahead. You will also experience joy, breakthrough, and divine empowerment as you align yourself with His will.

As you read this book, I encourage you to open your heart to God's voice and guidance. Reflect on the biblical examples of those who accepted their mantles and allow their stories to inspire and equip you. Review your journey, documenting the lessons, struggles, and victories. Accepting your mantle is not the end of the story—it is the beginning of a lifelong journey of faith and obedience. This journey will leave a lasting impact on you and those you are called to serve. Remember, you are not walking this path alone. God is with you, empowering you every step of the way.

Let us step forward together into God's extraordinary plans for our lives.

Chapter 1: Examples of Accepted Mantles in the Bible

When we speak of a mantle, we refer to the divine calling, responsibility, or authority God bestows upon a person. Accepting a mantle is not simply stepping into a role—it is embracing the weight of God's purpose and committing to His plan, often in the face of challenges and uncertainty. Throughout Scripture, we find powerful examples of individuals who accepted their mantles, sometimes reluctantly but always with transformative results. Let us explore a few of these stories and the lessons we can draw from them.

Elisha: The Mantle of Prophetic Authority

One of the most direct examples of a mantle being passed is found in the story of Elijah and Elisha. In 2 Kings 2:13-15, Elijah is taken to heaven in a whirlwind, leaving behind his physical mantle—a symbol of his prophetic authority. Elisha picks up this mantle, stepping into the role of Israel's prophet.

Elisha's acceptance of the mantle was not immediate. His journey began when Elijah threw the mantle over him while plowing a field (1 Kings 19:19-21). This act signified a calling, but Elisha had to make a choice. He left everything behind—his family, his livelihood—to follow Elijah. When we speak of a mantle, we refer to the divine calling, responsibility, or authority God bestows upon a person. Accepting a mantle is not simply stepping into a role—it is embracing the weight of God's purpose and committing to His plan, often in the face of challenges and uncertainty. Throughout Scripture, we find powerful examples of individuals who accepted their mantles, sometimes reluctantly but always with transformative results. Let us explore a few of these stories and the lessons we can draw from them.

Elisha: The Mantle of Prophetic Authority

One of the most direct examples of a mantle being passed is found in the story of Elijah and Elisha. In 2 Kings 2:13-15, Elijah is taken to heaven in a whirlwind, leaving behind his physical mantle—a symbol of his prophetic authority. Elisha picks up this mantle, stepping into the role of Israel's prophet.

Elisha's acceptance of the mantle was not immediate. His journey began when Elijah threw the mantle over him while plowing a field (1 Kings 19:19-21). This act signified a calling, but Elisha had to make a choice. He left everything behind—his family, his livelihood—to follow Elijah.

Lessons from Elisha's Mantle:
- Accepting a mantle often requires sacrifice. Elisha left his comfort zone to walk in God's calling.
- The transfer of the mantle signifies preparation. Elisha spent years under Elijah's mentorship, learning before stepping into full authority.
- Stepping into the mantle brings empowerment. After accepting the mantle, Elisha performed miracles, starting with parting the Jordan River.

Moses and Joshua: Leadership Passed Down

Moses led the Israelites out of Egypt and through the wilderness, but he was not permitted to enter the Promised Land. That responsibility fell to Joshua, his successor. In Deuteronomy 34:9, we read that Joshua was "filled with the spirit of wisdom because Moses had laid his hands on him."

Joshua's acceptance of the mantle required immense faith. The Israelites were challenging to lead, and stepping into Moses' shoes was no small task. However, Joshua rose to the occasion, trusting God's promise: *"As I was with Moses so that I will be with you"* (Joshua 1:5).

Lessons from Joshua's Mantle:

- God equips those He calls. Joshua's wisdom and courage came from God, not his strength.
- The mantle may involve leading others through challenges. Joshua faced battles, doubts, and internal struggles among the people.
- Faithfulness to God's instructions is critical. Joshua succeeded because he obeyed God, even when the tasks seemed impossible.

David: Anointed for Kingship

David's mantle was revealed long before he stepped into his role as king. In 1 Samuel 16:13, the prophet Samuel anointed David as king while he was still a shepherd boy. David's journey to the throne was marked by trials—persecution from Saul, battles, and personal failures—but he remained steadfast in his calling.

David's acceptance of his mantle highlights the process between anointed and appointed. Though God chose him, David had to wait for the right time to assume his position. During this waiting period, he grew character, learned to trust God, and developed as a leader.

Lessons from David's Mantle:

- God often calls the unlikely. David was his family's youngest and least significant, yet God chose him to lead Israel.
- The waiting period is a time of preparation. David learned humility and reliance on God during his years of waiting.
- Even with a mantle, failures can happen. David made mistakes, but his heart of repentance kept him aligned with God's purpose.

Mary: The Call to Birth the Savior

Perhaps one of the most profound examples of a mantle is Mary's calling to be the mother of Jesus. In Luke 1:26-38, the angel Gabriel announced God's plan to Mary, who responded with remarkable faith: *"I am the Lord's servant. May your word to me be fulfilled."*
Mary's acceptance of this mantle required immense courage. She faced potential shame, misunderstanding, and rejection but trusted God's plan. Her obedience paved the way for the greatest act of redemption in history.

Lessons from Mary's Mantle:
- Saying "yes" to God's mantle may lead to challenges, but His grace is sufficient.

- Faith is the foundation of accepting a mantle. Mary trusted God's word despite the unknown.
- Your mantle may impact generations. Mary's obedience brought salvation to the world through Jesus Christ.

Jesus: The Ultimate Mantle

Finally, we must consider Jesus Himself. He carried the ultimate mantle—to save humanity through His death and resurrection. Jesus accepted this mantle willingly, saying in John 10:18: *"No one takes it from me, but I lay it down of my own accord."*
Jesus' journey was marked by rejection, suffering, and sacrifice, yet He fulfilled His calling perfectly. His obedience is the ultimate example for us as we accept our mantles.

Lessons from Jesus' Mantle:
- The mantle often involves sacrifice. Jesus gave His life for the sake of humanity.
- Obedience to God is non-negotiable. Jesus submitted fully to the Father's will, even in the Garden of Gethsemane.
- The mantle carries eternal significance. Jesus' obedience opened the door to salvation for all who believe.

Each of these biblical examples reveals unique aspects of what it means to accept a mantle. Whether it is Elisha's prophetic authority, Joshua's leadership, David's kingship, Mary's obedience, or Jesus' ultimate sacrifice, we see that a mantle is both a privilege and a responsibility. It often involves challenges, but God's grace, guidance, and empowerment are always present.

As you reflect on these stories, ask yourself: What mantle has God placed on your life? What sacrifices might He be calling you to make? Furthermore, how can you step into your mantle with faith, courage, and obedience?

God's Word assures us that He will never leave or forsake us. The same God who empowered Elisha, Joshua, David, Mary, and Jesus walks with you as you accept your mantle. Will you trust Him with your journey?

Chapter 2: Types of Mantles

God's calling is as unique as the individual He entrusts with it. Just as the Bible presents various examples of mantles—representing different roles, responsibilities, and anointings—modern believers are called to fulfill diverse assignments within the kingdom of God. A mantle is not limited to a specific role like preaching or prophecy; it encompasses every divine purpose God assigns to advance His will on earth.

TYPES OF MANTLES

This chapter explores the types of mantles found in Scripture and how they apply to today's callings. Understanding your mantle is crucial to walking confidently in your assignment and recognizing the weight of the responsibility God has given you.

Prophetic Mantle

The prophetic mantle is a calling to speak God's truth, reveal His will, and guide His people. Those who carry this mantle often have a heightened sensitivity to God's voice and a responsibility to declare His messages, even in the face of opposition. Elijah and Elisha are prime examples of individuals who bore the prophetic mantle (1 Kings 19:19; 2 Kings 2:13-15). This mantle often requires boldness, discernment, and intimacy with God.

Characteristics of a Prophetic Mantle:
- Clear communication with God through visions, dreams, or direct revelation.
- A calling to confront sin and lead people back to God.
- A role in providing direction and encouragement to God's people.

Modern Application:
- Prophetic ministry in churches.
- Intercessors and spiritual counselors.

Leadership Mantle

The leadership mantle involves guiding, organizing, and overseeing others according to God's direction. Those called to this mantle are often entrusted with responsibilities that require vision, courage, and wisdom. Moses, Joshua, and Deborah are biblical examples of leaders who carried this mantle.

Characteristics of a Leadership Mantle:
- A calling to lead people toward a God-given goal or promise.
- Strength in decision-making and managing conflict.
- A heart of service and humility.

Modern Application:
- Pastors, church leaders, and organizational heads.
- Community leaders who advocate for justice and righteousness

Priestly Mantle

The priestly mantle is a calling to minister to God through worship, intercession, and teaching. Those with this mantle often act as spiritual mediators, bridging the gap between God and His people. Aaron, the first high priest, and his descendants were specifically called to carry this mantle (Exodus 28:1-3).

Characteristics of a Priestly Mantle:

- A heart for worship and intercession.
- A role in teaching and instructing others in God's Word.
- A deep commitment to holiness and consecration.

Modern Application:
- Worship leaders, prayer warriors, and Bible teachers.
- Those called to spiritual caregiving, such as chaplains or counselors.

Evangelistic Mantle

The evangelistic mantle is a calling to share the gospel, bringing the message of salvation to those who have not heard or accepted it. Paul and Timothy carried this mantle, dedicating their lives to spreading the good news to the gentiles (2 Timothy 4:5).

Characteristics of an Evangelistic Mantle:
- A passion for reaching the lost.
- Boldness and creativity in sharing the gospel.
- A willingness to endure challenges to advance God's kingdom.

Modern Application:
- Evangelists, missionaries, and outreach coordinators.
- Everday believers who witness to those in the communities and workplaces.

Mantle of Healing

The mantle of healing is a calling to bring physical, emotional, or spiritual restoration to others through the power of God. Jesus operated in this mantle throughout His ministry and commissioned His disciples to do the same (Matthew 10:8).

Characteristics of a Healing Mantle:
- A gift of faith and the ability to intercede for miracles.
- Compassion for the sick, broken, and oppressed.
- A heart for restoring wholeness in others.

Modern Application:
- Medical professionals who see their work as ministry.
- Those gifted with healing ministries in churches.

Mantle of Wisdom

The mantle of wisdom is a calling to provide guidance, counsel, and solutions grounded in God's truth. Solomon exemplifies this mantle, famously asking God for wisdom to lead His people (1 Kings 3:9-12).

Characteristics of a Wisdom Mantle:
- The ability to discern and apply God's principles in complex situations.
- A calling to mentor, advise, or lead others in godly decision-making.
- A reputation for integrity and understanding.

Modern Application:
- Counselors, mentors, and advisors.
- Those gifted in conflict resolution or strategic planning.

Marketplace Mantle

The marketplace mantle is a calling to operate in business, economics, or other professional fields in a way that glorifies God. Joseph carried this mantle, using his administrative skills to save Egypt and his family during a famine (Genesis 41:39-57).

Characteristics of a Marketplace Mantle:
- Excellence in professional skills and integrity.
- A commitment to honoring God in secular spaces.
- A heart for using resources to support God's kingdom.

Modern Application:
- Christian entrepreneurs, business leaders and professionals.

- Those called to influence culture through media, technology, or the arts.

Mantle of Intercession

The mantle of intercession is a calling to stand in the gap through persistent prayer on behalf of others. This mantle requires spiritual sensitivity, perseverance, and a heart for God's will. Daniel exemplified this mantle through his steadfast prayer life (Daniel 6:10).

Characteristics of an Intercession Mantle:
- A deep burden for prayer and spiritual warfare.
- The ability to discern spiritual needs and pray effectively.
- A heart for advocating for others before God.

Modern Application:
- Prayer warriors and intercessors in the church.
- Those called to lead prayer ministries or movements.

Discerning Your Mantle

Recognizing your mantle is an essential part of walking in your calling. Here are some steps to discern the mantle God has placed on your life:

1. Pray for Clarity: Ask God to reveal His specific purpose for you.

2. Reflect on Your Gifts: Consider the talents, skills, and passions God has given you.

3. Seek Confirmation: Look for confirmation through Scripture, prayer, and godly counsel.

4. Watch for Fruit: Identify where your efforts produce impact and align with God's will.

Embracing Your Mantle

No matter what mantle God has placed on your life, it is vital to embrace it with faith and humility. Each mantle is equally valuable in advancing God's kingdom, whether it involves leading a congregation, working in a professional field, or quietly interceding in prayer.

God has uniquely equipped you for your mantle and will provide everything you need to fulfill it. Trust in His guidance, align yourself with His will, and walk boldly in His calling on your life.

Chapter 3:
The Process Begins—
The Downloading Has Begun

Accepting the mantle is the first step; now, the journey truly begins. This stage, often referred to as "the downloading process," is when God starts to pour into you the wisdom, instruction, and spiritual resources you need to walk in your calling. Just as a phone receives updates to function effectively, you, too, require divine downloads to align with God's plans.

The downloading process is not instant but ongoing, requiring patience, surrender, and trust. During this time, God works through external circumstances and internally, preparing your heart, mind, and spirit for the assignment ahead. Let us explore what this process entails and how you can embrace it.

1. **Expect Loneliness and Separation**

    When God begins to download His plans into your life, He often separates you from distractions and influences that might hinder your ability to hear His voice. This season of separation can feel isolating, but it is purposeful. God cultivates intimacy with you in the stillness, sharpening your ability to discern His will.

Consider Jesus, who withdrew to the wilderness for 40 days before beginning His ministry (Matthew 4:1-11). During that time, He fasted, prayed, and faced temptation, but He emerged empowered by the Spirit. Similarly, Moses spent 40 years in the desert before God called him to lead Israel, and Paul spent time in Arabia before beginning his missionary work (Galatians 1:17).

What You Should Do in This Season:
- Embrace the quiet. Use this time to deepen your relationship with God through prayer and worship.
- Trust the process. Understand that separation is a tool for refinement, not rejection.
- Stay focused. Avoid the temptation to fill the silence with unnecessary noise or distractions.

2. **The Quiet Times: Learning to Hear God's Voice**

In the downloading process, God often speaks in whispers rather than shouts. During the quiet times, you learn to tune your ears to His voice. Hearing God is foundational to walking in your mantle because His guidance will direct every step of your journey. Elijah experienced this in 1 Kings 19:11-12. Elijah heard God softly after a dramatic display of wind, earthquake, and fire. This teaches us that while God can move in grand ways, His most straightforward guidance often comes in moments of stillness.

Practical Steps to Hear God's Voice:
- **Meditate on Scripture**: The Word of God is His voice. Spend time studying it, allowing it to guide your thoughts and actions.
- **Pray Intentionally**: Speak to God, but also take time to listen. Silence in prayer is as vital as speaking.
- **Journal Your Thoughts**: Write down what you sense God is saying. Over time, you will notice patterns of His direction and encouragement.

3. **The Role of Fasting and Prayer**

Fasting is an assertive spiritual discipline that enhances your ability to hear from God. When you deny your physical desires, you create space for spiritual clarity. Daniel fasted for understanding (Daniel 10:2-3), Esther fasted for deliverance

(Esther 4:16), and Jesus fasted for empowerment (Matthew 4:2). Fasting aligns your spirit with God's will during the downloading process and strengthens your ability to resist distractions and temptations. Prayer, paired with fasting, becomes a direct line to the Father, allowing you to receive His downloads with clarity and confidence.

Benefits of Fasting and Prayer:
- Heightened spiritual sensitivity.
- Greater focus on God's voice and purpose.
- Strengthened discipline and self-control.

How to Begin:
- Choose a fast that aligns with your physical and spiritual needs (e.g., a Daniel fast, partial fast, or complete fast).
- Set a purpose for your fast—what are you seeking from God?
- Commit to prayer and scripture reading during your fasting period.

4. **Facing Resistance**

The downloading process often comes with resistance. The enemy knows the power of a fully equipped believer, so he will try to interrupt your process. Distractions, doubts, and even unexpected challenges may arise to derail your focus.

My own experience is a testimony to this reality. Shortly after accepting my mantle, I found myself in a hospital, undergoing two surgeries in less than two weeks. Physically, I was drained, and spiritually, the enemy tried to convince me that I was too weak to be used by God. Nevertheless, even in the hospital bed, I sensed God downloading into me a greater understanding of perseverance and reliance on His strength. What felt like an attack was preparation.

How to Overcome Resistance:
- **Stay Anchored in Faith**: Remember that God is with you, even amid trials.
- **Declare Victory**: Speak God's promises over your situation, knowing the enemy's attacks are temporary.
- **Seek Support**: Surround yourself with spiritual mentors and prayer warriors who can intercede.

5. **Receiving Revelation and Instruction**

As the downloading continues, you will receive revelation about your assignment. God may reveal His plans through scripture, prayer, dreams, visions, or even conversations with others. These moments of clarity are like puzzle pieces that, over time, form a complete picture of your purpose.

Jeremiah 33:3 says, *"Call to me, and I will answer you and tell you great and unsearchable things you do not know."* God delights in revealing His plans to those who seek Him earnestly. Stay expectant and open to His voice.

6. **The Transformation of Your Character**

    During the downloading process, God is not just preparing you for your assignment; He is also preparing your heart. The mantle requires skill, humility, patience, and faith. God uses this time to refine your character, removing anything hindering your ability to fulfill your calling.

    Joseph's story is a powerful example. After receiving dreams of his destiny, he endured betrayal, slavery, and imprisonment before stepping into his role as Egypt's leader (Genesis 37-50). Each trial shaped him into the man God needed him to be.

    Questions for Reflection:
    - What areas of my character is God refining?
    - How can I surrender to the process instead of resisting it?
    - What lessons is God teaching me through my current circumstances?

Trust the Process

The downloading process is a sacred time of preparation, refinement, and revelation. While it may feel uncomfortable, remember that God equips you with something greater than you can imagine. Embrace the loneliness, quiet times, fasting, and even the resistance, knowing they are all part of His divine plan.

Trust that God, who began a good work in you, will complete it (Philippians 1:6). This is just the beginning of your journey with the mantle. Stay open, stay faithful, and watch as God prepares you to walk fully in His calling.

Chapter 4: Hearing God's Voice

Hearing God's voice is essential for walking in your mantle. It is the foundation upon which your calling is built. Without hearing from God, it is impossible to fully understand, pursue, or fulfill the purpose He has placed on your life. God speaks to us in many ways, and learning to recognize and respond to His voice is a skill that develops with time, intimacy, and practice.

In this chapter, we will explore how God speaks, the barriers that can hinder our ability to hear Him, and the steps we can take to cultivate a relationship where His voice becomes clear and unmistakable.

How God Speaks

The Bible reveals that God communicates with His people in various ways. He is not a distant deity but a loving Father who desires to guide and instruct us. Here are some of the primary ways God speaks:

1. **Through His Word (The Bible)**: God's Word is His primary means of communication. Scripture is living and active, capable of speaking directly to your situation (Hebrews 4:12). When you read the Bible prayerfully, God reveals His truth, gives direction, and provides reassurance.
   Example:
   - Psalm 119:105: *"Your word is a lamp to my feet and a light to my path."*
   - Jesus used Scripture to combat temptation in the wilderness (Matthew 4:1-11).

2. **Through the Holy Spirit**: The Holy Spirit is the still, small voice that speaks to your heart, guiding and convicting you. Jesus promised that the Spirit would teach us everything and remind us of His words (John 14:26).

Example:
- Acts 13:2: The Holy Spirit spoke to the church in Antioch, instructing them to set apart Barnabas and Saul for ministry.

3. **Through Prayer and Meditation**: Prayer is a two-way conversation. While we often focus on speaking to God, listening is equally important. In moments of stillness, God impresses His will on our hearts.

Example:
- Jeremiah 33:3: *"Call to me and I will answer you and tell you great and unsearchable things you do not know."*

4. **Through Circumstances**: God can use life events to direct your steps. Open doors, closed doors, and divine timing often reveal His will.

Example:
- Jonah's detour in the belly of the fish was God's way of redirecting him to fulfill his calling (Jonah 1-3).

5. **Through Others**: God often speaks through spiritual leaders, mentors, or even unexpected individuals. He can use a word of encouragement, correction, or prophecy to confirm His plans for you.

Example:
- Nathan confronted David about his sin, delivering God's message of judgment and grace (2 Samuel 12).

6. **Through Dreams and Visions**: God sometimes communicates through supernatural means, such as dreams and visions. These moments often come with specific instructions or insights about your calling.

Example:
- Joseph received dreams that revealed his future leadership (Genesis 37:5-11).
- Peter had a vision that led to including Gentiles in the faith (Acts 10).

Barriers to Hearing God's Voice

Hearing God's voice requires intentionality, but barriers can hinder this process. Identifying and overcoming these obstacles is critical to maintaining clarity and connection with Him.

1. **Sin**

    Sin creates a barrier between you and God. Unrepented sin dulls your spiritual senses, making it harder to discern His voice.
    - Isaiah 59:2: *"But your iniquities have separated you from your God; your sins have hidden his face from you so that he will not hear."*

    Solution: Confess and repent your sins, trusting in God's forgiveness.

2. **Distractions**

In a world filled with noise—social media, responsibilities, and worries—it is easy to lose focus. Distractions drown out God's voice.

- Luke 10:40-42: Martha was distracted by her tasks while Mary sat at Jesus' feet and listened.

Solution: Prioritize quiet time with God, free from interruptions.

3. **Impatience**

We often want immediate answers, but God speaks in His timing. Impatience can lead us to make decisions without waiting for His guidance.

- Psalm 27:14: *"Wait for the Lord; be strong and take heart and wait for the Lord."*

Solution: Trust in God's timing and remain steadfast in prayer.

4. **Doubt**

Questioning whether God is speaking can cause you to dismiss His voice.

- James 1:6: *"But when you ask, you must believe and not doubt, because the one who doubts is like a wave of the s ea, blown and tossed by the wind."*

Solution: Pray for faith and discernment, trusting God's desire to speak to you.

Cultivating a Life of Hearing God's Voice

1. **Create Space for God**

    Dedicate time each day to study Scripture, pray, and meditate. This consistency trains your spirit to recognize His voice.

2. **Practice Obedience**

    When you hear God's voice, act on it. Obedience strengthens your ability to hear Him more clearly.
    - John 10:27: *"My sheep listen to my voice; I know them, and they follow me."*

3. **Test What You Hear**

    Not every voice is from God. Test what you hear against Scripture, seek wise counsel, and seek confirmation through prayer and circumstances.
    - 1 John 4:1: *"Dear friends, do not believe every spirit, but test the spirits to see whether they are from God."*

4. **Stay in Community**

    Surround yourself with believers who encourage and support your walk. They can offer discernment and accountability.

5. **Be Patient in the Process**

    Learning to hear God's voice takes time. Be patient with yourself and trust that God is teaching you.

A Personal Testimony

I remember a time when I felt desperate to hear God's voice. After accepting my mantle, I entered a season of uncertainty, unsure of the next steps. I questioned whether God was speaking at all. However, I began to hear Him more clearly than ever in the stillness . He reminded me that my circumstances did not disqualify me and that He equipped me even in my weakness.

Through prayer, scripture, and moments of quiet reflection, I realized that God had been speaking all along—I just needed to quiet my mind and focus on Him.

Leaning Into God's Voice

Hearing God's voice is not reserved for a select few; it is a gift available to every believer. God desires a relationship with you, one where communication flows freely. You will find clarity, confidence, and peace in your journey as you learn to discern His voice.

Be encouraged: God is always speaking.

Your job is to listen.

Create space, remove barriers, and trust that the One who called you is faithful to guide you.

The more you lean into Him, the clearer His voice will become.

Chapter 5: When People Don't Understand

Accepting the mantle that God has placed on your life is a transformative and deeply personal experience. However, one of the greatest challenges of walking in your calling is realizing that not everyone will understand or support what God is doing in you. This lack of understanding can come from friends, family, coworkers, or even other believers. It can leave you feeling isolated, misunderstood, and discouraged.

But you are not alone. Scripture is full of examples of individuals who faced similar struggles. Their stories remind us that obedience to God's call is not about seeking the approval of others but about aligning yourself with His will. In this chapter, we'll explore why people may not understand your journey, how to handle their reactions, and how to stay faithful to your mantle despite opposition.

Why People Don't Understand

1. **They Lack Spiritual Insight**: Spiritual matters are not always discernible to those who are not walking closely with God. Your calling may seem strange, impractical, or even unnecessary to someone who does not share your faith or understanding of God's voice.
    - *"The person without the Spirit does not accept the things that come from the Spirit of God but considers them foolishness, and cannot understand them because they are discerned only through the Spirit"* (1 Corinthians 2:14).

2. **They Project Their Fears or Limitations**: Sometimes people's misunderstanding stems from their own fears or insecurities. They may project their doubts onto you, questioning whether you're capable of fulfilling the calling or whether it's worth the sacrifices.

3. **They Are Not Called to Your Assignment**: Your mantle is uniquely yours. God has given you a vision and purpose that others may not see or relate to because it is not their calling. Just as Joseph's brothers couldn't comprehend his dreams (Genesis 37:5-11), others may struggle to understand what God has revealed to you.

4. **The Enemy Sows Division**: Spiritual opposition can manifest through misunderstanding and conflict. The enemy will use others' doubts or criticisms to discourage you and distract you from your calling.

Biblical Examples of Misunderstanding

1. **Joseph's Brothers**: When Joseph shared his God-given dreams with his brothers, they became jealous and resentful. They couldn't see the divine purpose behind Joseph's calling and instead sought to destroy it (Genesis 37:18-20).

    Lesson: Be discerning about when and with whom to share your vision. Not everyone is ready to hear it or support it.

2. **David and His Family**: When the prophet Samuel anointed David as king, even David's father didn't initially see him as worthy. Later, when David volunteered to fight Goliath, his brother Eliab mocked him, accusing him of arrogance (1 Samuel 17:28).

Lesson: God's choice often defies human expectations. Don't let others' opinions shake your confidence in God's calling.

3. **Jesus and His Hometown**: Even Jesus faced rejection from those closest to Him. In Nazareth, people dismissed Him as merely the carpenter's son and questioned His authority (Matthew 13:54-57).

Lesson: Familiarity can breed contempt. Those who think they know you well may struggle to see you through the lens of your calling.

How to Handle Misunderstanding
1. **Stay Rooted in Your Identity**
Your identity is not defined by others' opinions but by God's calling on your life. Remember who you are in Christ and what He has spoken over you.
- *"But you are a chosen people, a royal priesthood, a holy nation, God's special possession"* (1 Peter 2:9).

2. **Guard Your Heart**
Misunderstanding can hurt, but don't let bitterness or resentment take root. Instead, pray for those who misunderstand you, asking God to soften their hearts and open their eyes to His work in your life.
- *"Above all else, guard your heart, for everything you do flows from it"* (Proverbs 4:23).

3. **Seek Wise Counsel**

   Surround yourself with people who understand your calling and can offer encouragement and guidance. Mentors, spiritual leaders, and trusted friends can help you stay grounded when others doubt you.

4. **Remain Obedient to God**

   Ultimately, your responsibility is to obey God, not to please people. Trust that He will honor your faithfulness, even if others do not.
   - *"Am I now trying to win the approval of human beings, or of God? Or am I trying to please people? If I were still trying to please people, I would not be a servant of Christ"* (Galatians 1:10).

5. **Recognize the Enemy's Tactics**

   Understand that misunderstanding is often a spiritual attack. Use prayer and the Word of God to combat discouragement and stay focused on your assignment.

Navigating Loneliness

One of the hardest aspects of misunderstanding is the loneliness it can bring. When people you love don't support or believe in your calling, it can feel isolating. But this loneliness can also be an opportunity to draw closer to God.

- **Lean on God's Presence**: When others don't understand,

God does. He is your greatest source of comfort and strength.
- **Find Community**: Seek out fellow believers who share your passion for God's work. They can provide the camaraderie and encouragement you need.
- **Trust the Journey**: Loneliness is often part of the refining process. Use this time to deepen your dependence on God and allow Him to strengthen your faith.

A Personal Reflection

When I accepted my mantle, I quickly realized that not everyone in my life understood what was happening. Some questioned why I was pursuing this path, while others doubted whether I was capable of fulfilling the calling. The misunderstanding wasn't malicious, but it was painful.

I felt emotionally vulnerable, and some around me couldn't comprehend how I still held onto my faith and calling in the midst of such difficulty. But in those quiet, lonely moments, I sensed God's reassurance. He reminded me that my calling wasn't dependent on others' understanding or approval—it was rooted in His purpose and power.

Encouragement for the Journey

When people don't understand your calling, remember these truths:
- You are chosen by God, and His plans for you are perfect.
- Rejection and misunderstanding are not a reflection of

your worth or ability but part of the journey.
- God will place the right people in your life to support and encourage you.
- Your faithfulness to God is what matters most.

Faith Over Approval

Misunderstanding is a natural part of walking in your mantle. It's a test of your resolve and faith. Will you trust God's voice over the opinions of others? Will you remain obedient even when you feel isolated or doubted?

Take heart in knowing that the One who called you understands you completely. His plans for your life are far greater than what others can see or imagine. Lean into His presence, and let His approval be enough.

Let this season of misunderstanding deepen your faith, sharpen your focus, and strengthen your commitment to the work God has called you to do. Remember: You don't need everyone to understand your journey—only God.

Chapter 6:
Aligning Yourself with God and His People

Walking in your mantle requires more than just a willingness to follow God's call; it requires intentional alignment with both God's will and the right people. Alignment is about positioning yourself spiritually, emotionally, and relationally to walk in obedience and purpose. It's a dynamic process that involves constant growth, discernment, and connection.

In this chapter, we'll explore what it means to align yourself with God and His people, why alignment is critical, and how to recognize when you're out of alignment.

What Does It Mean to Align with God?
Alignment with God means syncing your heart, mind, and actions with His will. It's about surrendering your desires and plans to embrace His purpose for your life. Jesus exemplified this alignment in the Garden of Gethsemane when He prayed, *"Not my will, but yours be done"* (Luke 22:42).

When you align with God:
1. **You Follow His Word**: Scripture becomes your guide, shaping your decisions and actions.
2. **You Submit to His Timing**: You trust that God's plans are perfect, even when they require patience.
3. **You Depend on His Strength**: You recognize that apart from Him, you can do nothing (John 15:5).
4. **You Embrace His Refinement**: You allow Him to mold your character, even through trials.

Practical Steps to Align with God
1. **Daily Devotion**
    Spend time each day in prayer, worship, and reading Scripture. These practices keep you connected to God's voice and help you discern His will.

- *"Your word is a lamp to my feet and a light to my path"* (Psalm 119:105).

2. **Obedience**

    Alignment requires action. When God gives you instructions, follow them, even when they don't make sense.
    - *"Do not merely listen to the word, and so deceive yourselves. Do what it says"* (James 1:22).

3. **Confession and Repentance**

    Sin disrupts alignment. Regularly examine your heart and ask God to reveal areas that need repentance.
    - *"If we confess our sins, he is faithful and just to forgive us our sins and to cleanse us from all unrighteousness"* (1 John 1:9).

4. **Surrender**

    Release control of your plans and trust that God's ways are higher than yours.
    - *"For my thoughts are not your thoughts, neither are your ways my ways," declares the Lord* (Isaiah 55:8).

The Role of People in Your Alignment

While alignment with God is foundational, He often works through people to guide, support, and challenge you. The right relationships can propel you forward in your calling, while the wrong ones can hinder your progress.

Why Relationships Matter

- **Support and Encouragement**: The right people provide strength when you feel weak.
- **Accountability**: Godly friends and mentors help keep you on track.
- **Wisdom and Perspective**: Others can offer insights that you may not see on your own.

How to Align with the Right People

1. **Seek a Spiritual Community**: Find a church or fellowship where you can grow spiritually and connect with like-minded believers. A strong spiritual community is essential for encouragement and accountability.
   - *"And let us consider how we may spur one another on toward love and good deeds, not giving up meeting together"* (Hebrews 10:24-25).

2. **Recognize God-Ordained Relationships**: Be discerning about the people God places in your life. Not every relationship is meant to last, but some are divinely appointed for your growth and purpose.
   - **Example**: Jonathan and David's friendship was a God-ordained relationship that provided mutual encouragement (1 Samuel 18:1-4)

3. **Honor Spiritual Authority**: Aligning with God often involves submitting to the leadership He has placed in your life, such as pastors, mentors, or spiritual advisors. These individuals are there to guide and equip you.
    - *"Obey your leaders and submit to them, for they are keeping watch over your souls"* (Hebrews 13:17).

4. **Guard Against Toxic Relationships**: Be cautious of people who distract or discourage you from your calling. Aligning with God sometimes requires letting go of relationships that are not aligned with His purpose.
    - *"Do not be misled: 'Bad company corrupts good character'"* (1 Corinthians 15:33).

Recognizing Misalignment

Misalignment often shows up as confusion, frustration, or stagnation in your walk with God. Signs of misalignment include:

- A lack of peace about your decisions.
- Struggling to hear God's voice or sense His direction.
- Feeling disconnected from your purpose.

When you recognize misalignment:
1. Pause and pray. Ask God to reveal where adjustments are needed.
2. Reevaluate your priorities and relationships.
3. Seek wise counsel to help you discern the next steps.

A Personal Reflection

In my journey, aligning with God and His people has been challenging and rewarding. After accepting the mantle, I experienced seasons where I felt alone and misunderstood. Yet, even in those moments of isolation, God spoke to me powerfully through the dreams and visions I experienced daily and nightly. These divine encounters were not just random occurrences but clear reminders of His presence, purpose, and plans for my life. They provided direction, reassurance, and a deeper understanding of His will, even when others couldn't see or understand what I was experiencing.

But God didn't leave me in isolation. He consistently brought the right people into my life—mentors, spiritual leaders, and friends—who encouraged, prayed for, and helped me stay focused. One of the most pivotal moments came during spiritual and physical weakness. After undergoing two surgeries in a short span, I found myself questioning my ability to carry out God's calling. Yet, even in that vulnerable state, the dreams and visions continued, affirming that God's hand was still on me. The prayers and support of my spiritual community reminded me that I wasn't walking this journey alone. They stood with me, helping me realign my focus on God's promises rather than my circumstances, and encouraged me to trust that His purpose for my life was far greater than any challenge I faced.

The Power of Alignment

When you are aligned with God and His people, you walk in divine strength and purpose. Alignment unlocks clarity, opens doors, and creates a flow of God's grace in your life. It doesn't mean the journey will be easy, but it ensures that you are equipped and supported to fulfill your mantle.

Reflection Questions

1. Are there areas in my life where I need to realign with God's will?
2. Who are the people God has placed in my life to support my calling?
3. Are there relationships or habits that may be pulling me out of alignment?

Walking in Alignment

Alignment is an ongoing process that requires intentionality and humility. By staying connected to God and surrounding yourself with the right people, you position yourself to walk confidently in your mantle.

Remember, God's plans are always greater than your own, and His people are a gift to help you fulfill them. Stay faithful, stay aligned, and watch as God works through you and those He has placed in your life to accomplish His divine purpose.

Chapter 7: The Importance of a Church Covering

One of the most critical aspects of walking in your mantle is understanding the value of being under a church covering. A church covering is more than just attending a weekly service—it's about submitting to spiritual leadership, being part of a faith community, and positioning yourself to grow and flourish under God's divine order.

In this chapter, we'll explore what a church covering is, why it's essential for your journey, and how it strengthens you as you walk in your calling.

What Is a Church Covering?

A church covering is the spiritual authority, guidance, and protection provided by the local church and its leadership. It reflects the biblical principle of being part of the body of Christ, where each member is connected and accountable to one another and to God-appointed leaders.
Paul describes this connection in 1 Corinthians 12:12-27, emphasizing that every believer is a vital part of the body, working together under Christ, the Head. Just as the body functions best when every part is aligned and connected, your spiritual journey flourishes when you are covered by a healthy church.

Key Aspects of a Church Covering:

1. **Spiritual Leadership**: God places pastors, elders, and leaders to guide, teach, and care for His people (Ephesians 4:11-13).

2. **Accountability**: Being part of a church helps you stay accountable in your faith and walk.

3. **Protection**: A covering provides spiritual protection against the attacks of the enemy.

Why Is a Church Covering Important?

1. **Biblical Mandate**
   Scripture emphasizes the importance of being connected to a spiritual community and submitting to God-appointed leaders.
   - *"Obey your leaders and submit to them, for they are keeping watch over your souls, as those who will have to give an account"* (Hebrews 13:17).

   God's design for the church is to serve as a place of spiritual nourishment, fellowship, and equipping for the work of ministry (Ephesians 4:12).

2. **Spiritual Growth**
   A church covering provides opportunities for discipleship, teaching, and mentorship. It's a space where you can grow in your knowledge of God, develop your gifts, and mature in your faith.
   - *"And let us consider how we may spur one another on toward love and good deeds, not giving up meeting together"* (Hebrews 10:24-25).

3. **Protection from Isolation**
   Walking in your mantle can feel isolating at times, but a church covering ensures you are never truly alone. The enemy often targets isolated believers, but a church community surrounds you with prayer, encouragement, and accountability.
   - *"Though one may be overpowered, two can defend*

themselves. A cord of three strands is not quickly broken" (Ecclesiastes 4:12).

4. **Confirmation and Guidance**
God often uses spiritual leaders to confirm your calling and provide direction. Their wisdom and experience can help you navigate challenges and avoid pitfalls.
- **Example**: Samuel's guidance in anointing and mentoring David prepared him for kingship (1 Samuel 16).

5. **Covering in Spiritual Warfare**
A church covering provides strength in spiritual battles. When you face attacks from the enemy, having a community that intercedes for you is invaluable.
- *"For where two or three gather in my name, there am I with them"* (Matthew 18:20).

What Happens Without a Church Covering?

Being without a church covering leaves you vulnerable. Just as a sheep without a shepherd is at risk of wandering and attack, a believer without a church covering is more susceptible to confusion, discouragement, and spiritual drift.

Signs of a Lack of Covering:
- Struggling to hear God's voice or discern His will.

- Feeling spiritually stagnant or disconnected.
- Facing repeated spiritual attacks without support.
- A tendency to drift into sin or compromise due to lack of accountability.

How to Find the Right Church Covering

1. **Pray for Guidance**
   Ask God to lead you to a church that aligns with His will for your life. Seek His wisdom in identifying a place where you can grow spiritually and serve effectively.
   - *"Trust in the Lord with all your heart and lean not on your own understanding; in all your ways submit to him, and he will make your paths straight"* (Proverbs 3:5-6).

2. **Look for Biblical Teaching**
   A healthy church is grounded in Scripture, teaching God's Word faithfully and consistently.

3. **Assess the Leadership**
   Look for leaders who model humility, integrity, and a heart for serving God's people. They should exhibit the qualities described in 1 Timothy 3:1-7 and Titus 1:5-9.

4. **Evaluate the Community**
   A church should feel welcoming and supportive, fostering fellowship and encouragement.

5. **Consider Your Calling**
    Find a church that supports and nurtures your calling. Some churches may have ministries or resources tailored to your specific gifts and passions.

Staying Aligned Under Your Church Covering

Once you are part of a church, it's important to stay aligned and connected. Being under a covering is not passive—it requires active participation and commitment.

1. **Be Accountable**: Submit to the authority of your church leaders and be open to correction and guidance.

2. **Serve Faithfully**: Use your gifts to serve the church and advance God's kingdom.
    - *"Each of you should use whatever gift you have received to serve others, as faithful stewards of God's grace"* (1 Peter 4:10).

3. **Pray for Your Leaders**: Church leaders face immense spiritual pressures. Lift them up in prayer and support their ministry.

4. **Stay Engaged**: Regularly attend services, participate in small groups, and build relationships within the community.

A Personal Reflection

I can personally attest to the power of a church covering. During one of the most challenging seasons of my life, I felt the prayers and support of my church community in a profound way. They surrounded me with encouragement, interceded on my behalf, and reminded me that I was not walking this journey alone.

Their covering gave me the strength to persevere, and their words of wisdom reaffirmed my calling. It was through their guidance that I realized the importance of staying connected to God and His people, even in times of trial.

The Power of a Covering

A church covering is one of God's greatest gifts to His people. It provides guidance, accountability, protection, and a sense of belonging as you walk in your mantle. No matter how strong or independent you feel, you cannot fulfill your calling alone. God designed the church to be a community where believers can grow, serve, and thrive together.

If you are under a church covering, cherish and honor it. If you are seeking one, trust that God will lead you to the right place. Remember, your mantle is not just about what you do for God; it's about who you walk with along the way.

THE IMPORTANCE OF A CHURCH COVERING

Align yourself with a church that helps you grow closer to God and empowers you to walk boldly in your calling. Under the safety and strength of a church covering, you will find the support and encouragement you need to fulfill the purpose God has placed on your life.

Chapter 8: Obedience Over Trends

In a world where trends dominate every facet of life—fashion, social media, business, and even ministry—it can be tempting to follow what's popular rather than what's purposeful. However, walking in your mantle requires unwavering obedience to God's call, even when it goes against the current of societal or cultural trends. Obedience to God is not about conforming to what's in style; it's about staying faithful to His eternal Word and unique plans for your life.

This chapter explores why obedience is more important than trends, how to recognize the subtle pull of conformity, and how to remain steadfast in your calling, even when it sets you apart.

The Priority of Obedience

Obedience is the cornerstone of fulfilling your mantle. When God calls you, He requires your "yes" to His will, even when it is uncomfortable, inconvenient, or countercultural. Scripture makes it clear that God values obedience over outward actions or sacrifices.

- *"To obey is better than sacrifice, and to heed is better than the fat of rams"* (1 Samuel 15:22).
- *"If you love me, keep my commands"* (John 14:15).

Obedience aligns your heart with God's, positioning you to walk in His power and authority. It is through obedience that you fulfill the specific assignment He has entrusted to you, rather than chasing fleeting trends that may appear successful but lack eternal significance.

The Danger of Following Trends

Trends are temporary by nature, constantly shifting with the preferences and priorities of the world. While trends may offer short-term relevance, they can pull you away from God's unique plan for your life if you're not discerning. Here are some of the dangers of following trends:

1. **Distraction from Your Purpose**:
   Trends often entice you to focus on what's popular rather than

what's purposeful. You risk diverting your energy from the work God has called you to do.

2. **Comparison and Competition**
Following trends can lead to unhealthy comparisons, making you feel inadequate or pressured to keep up with others.
- *"Each one should test their own actions. Then they can take pride in themselves alone, without comparing themselves to someone else"* (Galatians 6:4).

3. **Loss of Authenticity**
When you prioritize trends, you may compromise your authenticity and unique identity in Christ, trying to fit into a mold that was never meant for you.

4. **Spiritual Drift**
Trends often cater to the flesh, not the Spirit. Pursuing them can cause you to drift from God's voice and will.
- *"Do not conform to the pattern of this world, but be transformed by the renewing of your mind"* (Romans 12:2).

Biblical Examples of Obedience Over Trends

1. **Noah's Ark**
Noah's obedience to God was radical and countercultural. Building an ark in the middle of dry land must have seemed

absurd to those around him, yet Noah trusted God's instructions over the opinions of others. His faithfulness saved his family and preserved humanity (Genesis 6-9).

Lesson: Obedience often requires you to act in faith, even when others don't understand or agree.

2. **Moses and the Israelites**

Moses obeyed God's call to lead the Israelites out of Egypt, even though he felt unqualified. He resisted the pressure to conform to Pharaoh's demands or follow the fear of the people.

- *"By faith he left Egypt, not fearing the king's anger; he persevered because he saw him who is invisible"* (Hebrews 11:27).

Lesson: Obedience requires courage to trust God's unseen plans over visible obstacles.

3. **Jesus' Ministry**

Jesus consistently chose obedience to the Father over societal expectations. From healing on the Sabbath to associating with sinners, His actions defied religious and cultural norms. His ultimate act of obedience was going to the cross, despite the agony it entailed.

- *"He humbled himself by becoming obedient to death—even death on a cross!"* (Philippians 2:8).

Lesson: Obedience may lead to sacrifice, but it fulfills God's eternal purpose.

How to Choose Obedience Over Trends

1. **Focus on God's Voice**
   Regularly seek God in prayer and through His Word to discern His specific instructions for your life. The clearer His voice becomes, the less appealing trends will be.
   - *"Whether you turn to the right or to the left, your ears will hear a voice behind you, saying, 'This is the way; walk in it'"* (Isaiah 30:21).

2. **Know Your Assignment**
   Understand your mantle and stay committed to it. When you are confident in your God-given purpose, you are less likely to be swayed by what others are doing.

3. **Resist the Fear of Missing Out (FOMO)**
   Trends often play on the fear of being left behind or irrelevant. Remind yourself that God's timing is perfect and that you are walking on His schedule, not the world's.
   - *"He has made everything beautiful in its time"* (Ecclesiastes 3:11).

4. **Cultivate Contentment**
   Contentment in God's plan protects you from the need to chase validation or success through trends. Trust that God's purpose for your life is enough.

- *"But godliness with contentment is great gain"* (1 Timothy 6:6).

5. **Stay Rooted in Community**
Surround yourself with people who value obedience to God over conformity to the world. A supportive spiritual community will encourage you to remain faithful to your calling.

Obedience Requires Sacrifice

Choosing obedience over trends often comes with a cost. You may face criticism, feel out of step with others, or miss opportunities that seem appealing in the moment. However, the rewards of obedience far outweigh the sacrifices.

- **Eternal Impact**: Obedience aligns your actions with God's eternal plans, creating a lasting legacy.
- **Peace and Joy**: Walking in God's will brings a deep sense of peace and fulfillment, regardless of external circumstances.
- **Divine Favor**: God honors those who trust Him enough to obey, even when it's difficult.

A Personal Reflection

In my own journey, I've felt the pull of trends—whether it was ministry strategies, career moves, or social expectations. There were moments when it seemed easier to follow what others were doing rather than what God had instructed me to do. But every time I veered off course, I felt the gentle conviction of the Holy Spirit reminding me that my obedience mattered more than my popularity or success.

One of the most profound lessons came during a season of personal trials. I was tempted to put my mantle aside and focus on survival. But God reminded me that even in my weakness, obedience was required. He showed me that my journey wasn't about following what others thought I should do but about trusting Him completely.

Faithfulness Over Fads

Trends will come and go, but God's Word remains forever. When you choose obedience over trends, you anchor your life in the unshakable foundation of His truth. Your mantle is not about blending in with the crowd but about standing apart for God's glory.

Remember, obedience may not always be easy, but it is always worth it. Trust that God's plans for your life are far greater than anything the world could offer. As you walk in obedience, you will experience the fullness of His blessings and fulfill the unique purpose He has for you.

Stay faithful. Stay obedient. And watch as God uses your life to make an eternal impact.

Journaling Section: Embrace the Process

As you walk in your mantle, embracing the process is essential. God uses every season, every trial, and every triumph to prepare you for His purpose. Journaling is a powerful tool for reflecting on what He's teaching you, tracking your growth, and staying connected to His voice. Use the prompts in this section to document your journey, process your emotions, and align your heart with God's plan.

1. **Recognizing the Call**
    Reflect on when you realized God was calling you to a specific mantle. Think about how it felt, what He spoke to your heart, and what confirmations you received.

Journal Prompt:
- When did you first sense God's call on your life?
- How did He confirm this call to you?
- What emotions did you experience when you accepted the mantle?

Scripture for Reflection:
- *"For we are God's handiwork, created in Christ Jesus to do good works, which God prepared in advance for us to do"* (Ephesians 2:10).

2. **The Challenges of the Process**

   Carrying your mantle is often marked by challenges—loneliness, misunderstanding, and moments of self-doubt. These challenges are not meant to break you but to refine you.

Journal Prompt:
- What challenges have you faced since accepting your mantle?
- How have these challenges shaped your character and strengthened your faith?
- What lessons has God taught you through these difficulties?

Scripture for Reflection:
- *"Consider it pure joy, my brothers and sisters, whenever you face trials of many kinds, because you know that the testing of your faith produces perseverance"* (James 1:2-3).

3. **Hearing God's Voice**

Hearing and discerning God's voice is foundational to fulfilling your mantle. Reflect on how He has spoken to you and how you have responded.

Journal Prompt:
- How has God been speaking to you during this season?
- What steps have you taken to cultivate a more profound ability to hear His voice?
- How have you acted on what He has revealed to you?

Scripture for Reflection:
- *"My sheep listen to my voice; I know them, and they follow me"* (John 10:27).

4. **Overcoming Misunderstanding**

It is natural to feel hurt or discouraged when others do not understand your calling. Use this space to process those emotions and seek God's perspective.

Journal Prompt:
- Who has misunderstood your calling, and how has it affected you?
- How have you sought to respond with grace and forgiveness?
- What has God revealed to you about walking in faith despite misunderstanding?

Scripture for Reflection:
- *"Am I now trying to win the approval of human beings, or*

God? Or am I trying to please people? If I were still trying to please people, I would not be a servant of Christ" (Galatians 1:10).

5. **Aligning Yourself with God**

   Alignment with God is an ongoing process that requires surrender and intentionality. Reflect on how you have been aligning yourself with His will and how He is guiding your steps.

   Journal Prompt:
   - What areas of your life need realignment with God's will?
   - How have you seen God's hand in guiding your decisions and actions?
   - What steps can you take to deepen your relationship with Him?

   Scripture for Reflection:
   - *"Trust in the Lord with all your heart and lean not on your understanding; in all your ways submit to him, and he will make your paths straight"* (Proverbs 3:5-6).

6. **The Role of Community and Covering**

   Reflect on the relationships God has placed in your life to support your journey. Consider how your church cover and community have impacted your growth.

Journal Prompt:
- Who are the people God has placed in your life to support your calling?
- How has your church covering encouraged and strengthened you?
- What role has spiritual accountability played in your journey?

Scripture for Reflection:
- *"As iron sharpens iron, so one person sharpens another"* (Proverbs 27:17).

7. **Obedience Over Trends**

Staying obedient to God's call often means resisting the pull of trends and societal expectations. Use this space to reflect on how you have prioritized obedience.

Journal Prompt:
- What trends or distractions have you felt tempted to follow, and how did you resist?
- How has obedience to God brought clarity or peace in your journey?
- What has God revealed about the importance of staying faithful to His unique plan for your life?

Scripture for Reflection:
- *"Do not conform to the pattern of this world, but be transformed by the renewing of your mind. Then you will be able to test and approve what God's will is—his good, pleasing, and perfect will"* (Romans 12:2).

8. **Celebrating the Victories**

God's faithfulness is evident in the big and small victories you experience along the way. Celebrate these moments as reminders of His provision and grace.

Journal Prompt:
- What victories has God brought you through since you began walking in your mantle?
- How have these moments strengthened your faith and confidence in Him?
- What gratitude do you want to express to God for His faithfulness?

Scripture for Reflection:
- *"To him who can do immeasurably more than all we ask or imagine, according to his power that is at work within us, to him be glory"* (Ephesians 3:20-21).

Prayer for Reflection

Use this prayer to guide your journaling process:

Heavenly Father, I thank You for your calling on my life. As I walk in this mantle, help me embrace the process, trust in Your timing, and lean on Your strength. Teach me through every challenge and refine my heart to align with Your will. Open my ears to hear Your voice, and help me to remain faithful, even when the journey is difficult. Surround me with the right people, and remind me daily of Your love and purpose for me. In Jesus' name, Amen.

Embrace the process, for it shapes you into the person God created you to be. Let this journaling section become a record of His faithfulness and a guide for the steps ahead.

Chapter 9:
The Attacks of the Enemy

When you accept the mantle God has placed on your life, you step into a divine purpose that threatens the enemy's agenda. Spiritual attacks are not a possibility—they are a certainty. The enemy knows the power of a surrendered and obedient servant of God and will stop at nothing to derail you. Understanding the nature of these attacks, recognizing them when they arise, and standing firm in your faith are essential to walking in victory.

In this chapter, we'll explore the enemy's tactics, the purpose behind his attacks, and how to guard yourself spiritually while continuing to walk boldly in your calling.

Why the Enemy Attacks

The devil's goal is simple: to oppose God's work. You become a target when you say "yes" to your mantle because you threaten his kingdom. Your calling carries the power to bring freedom, healing, and transformation to others, which the enemy cannot allow to go unchallenged.

- *"The thief comes only to steal, kill, and destroy"* (John 10:10).
- *"Be alert and of sober mind. Your enemy, the devil, prowls around like a roaring lion looking for someone to devour"* (1 Peter 5:8).

The enemy attacks to:
1. **Discourage You**: He plants seeds of doubt, fear, and insecurity to make you question your ability to fulfill your calling.
2. **Distract You**: He uses worldly concerns, busyness, and good opportunities to distract you from God's specific purpose.
3. **Divide You**: He sows discord in relationships to isolate you from your support system and spiritual community.
4. **Destroy Your Faith**: He targets your trust in God, hoping to weaken your reliance on Him.

Recognizing the Enemy's Tactics

1. **Physical Attacks**
   Sometimes, the enemy targets your body through sickness, fatigue, or unexpected physical challenges. These attacks weaken your resolve and distract you from your purpose.

   Example: My own experience with two surgeries in less than two weeks is a testimony of the enemy's attempt to discourage and derail me. In those moments of physical weakness, the enemy whispered lies, trying to convince me that I was too broken to be used by God. But even in that hospital bed, I chose to declare that my body and life belonged to God.

2. **Emotional and Mental Battles**
   The enemy often attacks the mind with thoughts of fear, inadequacy, or unworthiness. He aims to make you doubt God's call on your life.
   - *"For God has not given us a spirit of fear, but of power and love and a sound mind"* (2 Timothy 1:7).

3. **Relational Strife**
   Relationships are the enemy's primary target because division weakens your support system. He may stir up misunderstandings, conflicts, or betrayals to isolate you
   - *"For our struggle is not against flesh and blood, but*

against the rulers, against the authorities, against the powers of this dark world" (Ephesians 6:12).

4. **Spiritual Attacks**

These may include doubts about your faith, confusion about hearing God's voice, or feelings of distance from Him. The enemy seeks to disconnect you from the very source of your strength.

Standing Firm Amid Attack

1. **Put on the Full Armor of God**

God provides spiritual armor to protect you against the enemy's schemes. Ephesians 6:10-18 outlines each piece:
- Belt of truth: Stand firm in God's Word
- Breastplate of righteousness: Live a life of integrity and holiness.
- Shoes of peace: Walk confidently in the gospel of peace.
- Shield of faith: Deflect the enemy's fiery darts of doubt and fear.
- Helmet of salvation: Protect your mind with the assurance of your salvation.
- Sword of the Spirit: Fight back with the Word of God.

Action Step: Memorize and meditate on Ephesians 6:10-18, and pray each morning for God's protection as you enter your day.

2. **Use the Power of Prayer**
   Prayer is your greatest weapon. It aligns you with God's will, strengthens your spirit, and pushes back the enemy. When Jesus was tempted in the wilderness, He countered every attack with God's Word and prayer (Matthew 4:1-11).

   Action Step: Develop a habit of consistent prayer, especially during moments of attack. Surround yourself with prayer warriors who can intercede on your behalf.

3. **Resist the Devil**
   Scripture promises that when you resist the devil, he will flee (James 4:7). Stand firm in your faith, speak God's promises aloud, and refuse to give in to fear or temptation.

   Action Step: Write down Scripture verses that remind you of God's power and victory. Declare them daily over your life.

4. **Stay Connected to the Community**
   Isolation is one of the enemy's favorite tactics. Surround yourself with a church covering, mentors, and friends who will support and encourage you.
   - *"Carry each other's burdens, and in this way you will fulfill the law of Christ"* (Galatians 6:2).

God's Purpose in the Attack

While the enemy's attacks are meant for harm, God uses them for good. Every trial is an opportunity for growth, refinement, and a more profound dependence on Him.

- **Joseph's Story**: What the enemy intended for evil, God used for good to save many lives (Genesis 50:20).
- **Paul's Thorn**: Paul's affliction kept him humble and dependent on God's grace (2 Corinthians 12:7-9).

When you face attacks, remember that they are a sign that you are on the right path. The enemy would not bother you if you did not threaten his kingdom.

Practical Ways to Prepare for Battle

1. **Worship Through the Storm**
   Worship shifts your focus from the problem to God, who is more significant than any challenge. Worship is also a weapon that confuses the enemy (2 Chronicles 20:22).

2. **Fast for Breakthrough**
   Fasting heightens your spiritual sensitivity and aligns you with God's power.

3. **Keep Moving Forward**
   The enemy wants to paralyze you with fear and doubt. Refuse to

A Personal Reflection

During my hospital stay, I realized the enemy was working overtime to stop me. He tried to weaken my body, disrupt my peace, and make me question my ability to fulfill my calling. Nevertheless, I fought back through prayer, worship, and the support of my spiritual community. Those two weeks became a defining moment in my faith journey, reminding me that God's plans cannot be thwarted, no matter how fierce the attack.

Victory is Yours

The enemy's attacks are actual, but so is the victory God has already secured for you. Remember that you are not fighting for victory—you are fighting from a place of victory. Jesus has already defeated the enemy on your behalf (Colossians 2:15).
Stay strong, stay vigilant, and stay rooted in God's Word. As you continue to walk in your mantle, trust that He will equip you to overcome every attack and fulfill His purpose for your life.

- *"No weapon forged against you will prevail, and you will refute every tongue that accuses you"* (Isaiah 54:17).

Chapter 10: Fully Accepting the Mantle God Has Placed on You

Accepting the mantle God has placed on your life is more than simply acknowledging His call—it is a wholehearted surrender to His purpose, an active step of faith, and a commitment to align every part of your life with His will. To fully accept your mantle, you must move beyond initial hesitation, face challenges head-on, and embrace the responsibility with humility and confidence. This chapter explores what it means to fully accept your mantle, using biblical examples and practical steps to guide you.

1. **Acknowledge the Call**

   The first step to fully accepting your mantle is acknowledging that God has called you. This may sound simple, but believing that God would choose you for such a significant purpose can be challenging. Many biblical figures struggled with this initial step, feeling unworthy or incapable.

   Example: Moses

   When God called Moses to deliver the Israelites from Egypt, Moses doubted his ability. He said, *"Who am I that I should go to Pharaoh and bring the Israelites out of Egypt?"* (Exodus 3:11). Yet God reassured him, *"I will be with you"* (Exodus 3:12).

   Action Step: Spend prayer, affirming that God has chosen you for this purpose. Meditate on Scriptures that confirm His calling, such as:
   - *"Before I formed you in the womb I knew you, before you were born I set you apart"* (Jeremiah 1:5).90

2. **Surrender Your Fears and Excuses**

   Fear and doubt are common when faced with the weight of a mantle. Fully accepting your mantle requires surrendering these fears to God and trusting His strength over your own.

   Example: Gideon
   Gideon initially doubted God's call to lead Israel against the Midianites, saying, *"Pardon me, my lord, but how can I save Israel? My clan is the weakest in Manasseh, and I am the least in my family"* (Judges 6:15). Despite his fear, Gideon obeyed, and God gave him the victory.

   Action Step: Identify your fears and surrender them to God in

prayer. Declare Scriptures like:
- *"For the Spirit God gave us does not make us timid, but gives us power, love, and self-discipline"* (2 Timothy 1:7).

3. **Submit to God's Refining Process**

Accepting your mantle often involves a season of preparation. This is where God refines your character, strengthens your faith, and equips you for the responsibilities ahead. Embrace this process, even when it feels uncomfortable or challenging.

Example: Joseph
Joseph was given a dream of his future leadership but spent years in slavery and prison before stepping into his mantle. These trials prepared him to lead with wisdom and humility (Genesis 37-50).

Action Step: Reflect on your trials and ask God to reveal how He is using them to prepare you. Trust that His refining process is necessary for your growth.
- *"Consider it pure joy, my brothers and sisters, whenever you face trials of many kinds, because you know that the testing of your faith produces perseverance"* (James 1:2-3).

4. **Take Action in Obedience**

Accepting your mantle requires active obedience. You must move beyond hearing God's call to taking tangible steps toward fulfilling it. Even small acts of obedience demonstrate your willingness to trust Him.

Example: Elisha
When Elijah threw his mantle over Elisha, Elisha immediately left his oxen and followed him (1 Kings 19:19-21). His action symbolized his total commitment to the prophetic calling.

Action Step: Ask God for the next step He wants you to take and follow through. Whether serving in your church, reaching out to a mentor, or starting a new project, obedience in small things leads to more significant assignments.

5. **Trust God's Provision and Power**

    God never gives you a mantle without equipping you to carry it. He provides the resources, wisdom, and strength you need. Fully accepting your mantle means trusting He will supply everything necessary to fulfill His purpose.

    Example: The Disciples
    When Jesus gave His disciples the Great Commission, He promised, *"And surely I am with you always, to the very end of the age"* (Matthew 28:20). The Holy Spirit empowered them to fulfill their calling (Acts 2).

    Action Step: Pray for God's provision and power to be evident in your life. Trust that He will supply everything you need.
    - *"And my God will meet all your needs according to the riches of his glory in Christ Jesus"* (Philippians 4:19).

6. **Surround Yourself with Godly Support**

    Carrying your mantle is not a solo journey. God often brings mentors, spiritual leaders, and supportive friends into your life to encourage and guide you. Fully accepting your mantle means being open to receiving their help.

    Example: Paul and Timothy
    Paul mentored Timothy, equipping him to carry his church leadership mantle. Paul's guidance and encouragement strengthened Timothy's faith (2 Timothy 1:6-7).

Action Step: Identify people in your life who can support and guide you. Build relationships with those who encourage your spiritual growth.

7. **Commit to Lifelong Faithfulness**

Your mantle is not a temporary role; it is a lifelong calling. Fully accepting it means committing to remain faithful to God, even when facing challenges or setbacks.

Example: Jesus
Jesus was faithful to His mantle until the end, fulfilling His purpose on the cross and declaring, *"It is finished"* (John 19:30).

Action Step: Pray for endurance and faithfulness in your calling. Reflect on Scriptures like:
- *"Let us run with perseverance the race marked out for us, fixing our eyes on Jesus, the pioneer and perfecter of faith"* (Hebrews 12:1-2)

Practical Steps to Fully Accept Your Mantle

1. **Pray for Confirmation**: Ask God to affirm your mantle through His Word, prayer, and godly counsel.

2. **Write It Down**: Journal what God has revealed about your calling.

3. **Set Goals**: Break down your mantle into actionable steps and commit to starting today.

4. **Stay Aligned**: Regularly spend time with God to ensure you remain in His will.

5. **Celebrate Progress**: Acknowledge milestones in your journey as evidence of God's faithfulness

A Prayer for Full Acceptance

Heavenly Father,

Thank You for choosing me to carry this mantle and trusting me with Your purpose. Help me to fully accept this calling, surrendering my fears, doubts, and excuses to You. Refine me through Your process, and equip me with everything I need to fulfill this assignment. Strengthen my faith, guide my steps, and align my heart with Your will. Surround me with the right people who will encourage and support me.

Lord, I commit to obeying You, trusting Your provision, and remaining faithful to this mantle for as long as You have called me to carry it. Let my life glorify You and bring others closer to Your kingdom. I declare that Your plans for my life will prevail. In Jesus' name, Amen.

Accepting your mantle is not a one-time decision—it is a daily commitment to walk in obedience, trust, and faith. Step into your calling boldly, knowing that God is with you every step of the way.

Walking Boldly in Your Mantle

You have accepted the mantle. You have said "yes" to God's calling in your life. You have stepped into a journey that is both challenging and rewarding, filled with seasons of refinement, revelation, and purpose. This book has guided you through the critical aspects of carrying your mantle—from understanding its biblical foundation to embracing the process, overcoming opposition, and staying aligned with God's will.

As you continue, remember that this journey is not about perfection but persistence. God does not call the qualified; He qualifies the called. He does not expect you to walk this path in your strength but invites you to rely on His grace and power every step of the way.

Critical Reminders for the Journey

1. **Your Calling is Unique**

    God has designed you for a purpose that no one else can fulfill. Do not compare your journey to others or feel pressured to follow trends. Stay focused on the assignment God has given you.

2. **The Process is Necessary**

    The seasons of waiting, trials, and refinement are not setbacks—they are opportunities for growth and preparation. Embrace the process, knowing that God equips you for what lies ahead.

3. **Opposition is a Sign of Progress**

    The enemy's attacks are not a sign that you are failing but that you are advancing God's kingdom. Stand firm, trusting that God has already secured your victory.

4. **Obedience is the Key to Success**

    True success is found in obeying God, even when difficult or unpopular. Your faithfulness matters more than the approval of others.

5. **Stay Connected to God and His People**
    Alignment with God and a strong church covering provide the support, guidance, and accountability you need to thrive. Surround yourself with people who encourage and sharpen your walk with God.

Moving Forward with Confidence

The road ahead will not always be easy, but it will always be worth it. You will experience God's presence in powerful ways as you carry your mantle. You will see His faithfulness as He opens doors, provides resources, and brings people into your life to support your journey. You will grow in faith, character, and spiritual authority, becoming the person God created you to be.

Remember, God's calling on your life is not just about you—it is about the lives you will impact, the souls you will touch, and the glory you will bring to His name. Your obedience can change lives, transform communities, and advance God's kingdom.

Prayer of Empowerment

Heavenly Father,

Thank You for choosing me to carry this mantle and trusting me with Your purpose. As I continue this journey, I ask for Your strength, wisdom, and guidance. Help me walk boldly, knowing that You go before me and Your plans for me are good. Strengthen me in moments of doubt, comfort me in seasons of loneliness, and empower me to stand firm against the enemy's attacks.

Lord, I surrender every part of my life to You. Align my heart with Your will, and let my steps be ordered by You. Surround me with the right people, and help me to stay connected to Your Word and Your presence. Let my life be a testimony of Your goodness and faithfulness. I declare that no weapon formed against me shall prosper and that Your purpose for my life will prevail.

As I move forward, I commit to obeying You above all else, trusting that Your plans are far greater than my own. Use me, Lord, for Your glory. Let my mantle bring honor to Your name and light to a world in need.

In Jesus' name, Amen.

Your Journey is Just Beginning

This is not the end of your story—it's the beginning of a lifelong journey of faith, obedience, and impact. Go forward boldly, knowing that the One who called you is faithful to complete the good work He has started in you (Philippians 1:6). You are chosen, equipped, and empowered for such a time as this.

Carry your mantle with confidence, courage, and unwavering faith. God is with you, and His plans for your life are greater than anything you could imagine. Walk boldly into the destiny He has prepared for you!

ABOUT THE AUTHOR

I am passionate about spreading the Gospel of Jesus Christ through Christian Education. With over 15 years of teaching experience, God has gifted me the ability to simplify complex principles and make them accessible to others. My personal journey of understanding the Bible and preachers' messages has shaped my teaching approach. I have experienced firsthand how God reveals His truth through dreams and visions, which has deepened my understanding of His word. In addition to my teaching ministry, I have been actively involved in church leadership for over two decades. Although I initially desired a more behind-the-scenes role, God redirected me to share His message actively. My educational background includes an associate's degree in early childhood education, a bachelor's degree in Birth-Kindergarten, and a master's degree in Birth-Kindergarten. I have also obtained certificates in community college instruction and autism and autism spectrum disorders. I hold a Doctoral degree in Christian Leadership, furthering my knowledge and expertise in this field.

www.ingramcontent.com/pod-product-compliance
Lightning Source LLC
Chambersburg PA
CBHW040926190426
43197CB00033B/108